# A 2024 CALENDAR

## A Tool for ESL Teachers

**CREATED BY:**
**LYNN RICHARDSON**

# 12

# MONTH ESL/ART
# LEARNING ACTIVITIES

# CONTENTS

# JANUARY

## CELEBRATING 2024 AROUND THE WORLD

Students will share how each of them celebrated or observed the 2024 New Year.

They will explore how New Year celebrations are conducted throughout the world and share their findings through visuals (drawings and paintings) and oral presentations.

National Geographic Kids is a website that provides a brief overview of how New Years is celebrated in different countries along with some important facts and figure.

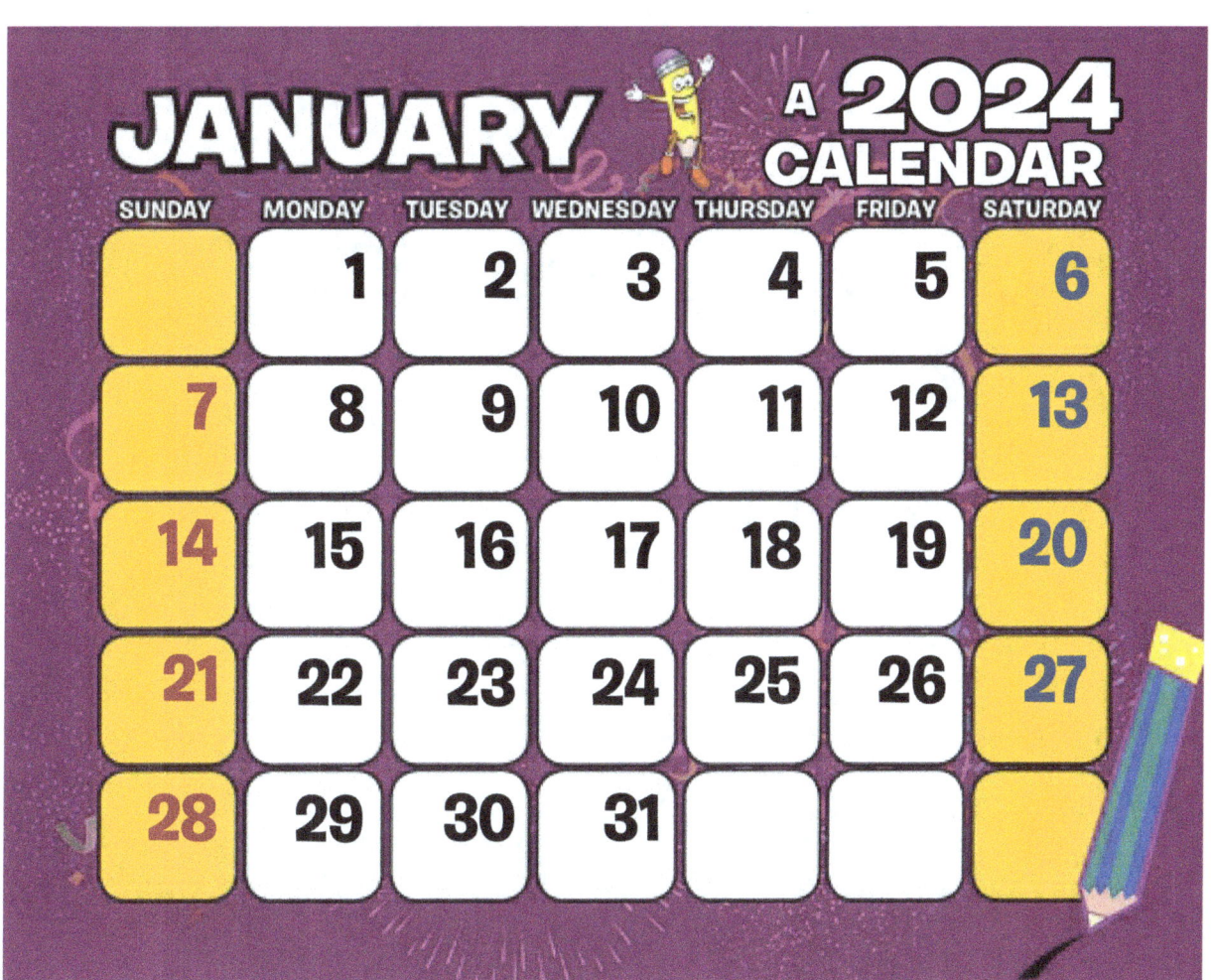

# JANUARY

## A 2024 CALENDAR

| SUNDAY | MONDAY | TUESDAY | WEDNESDAY | THURSDAY | FRIDAY | SATURDAY |
|--------|--------|---------|-----------|----------|--------|----------|
|        | 1      | 2       | 3         | 4        | 5      | 6        |
| 7      | 8      | 9       | 10        | 11       | 12     | 13       |
| 14     | 15     | 16      | 17        | 18       | 19     | 20       |
| 21     | 22     | 23      | 24        | 25       | 26     | 27       |
| 28     | 29     | 30      | 31        |          |        |          |

# FEBRUARY

## GUNG HAY FAT CHOY DESIGNS

Students learn that February is the month of love and February is also the month of Gung Hay Fat Choy. Gung Hay Fat Choy is a special holiday which is celebrated by Asians all over the world. Kids-World-Travel-Guide.com is a website which includes information on Chinese New Year traditions and celebrations such as dragon dances, lion dances, gift exchanges, fireworks, and more. This year will be The Year Of The Dragon which will be observed on February 10th, 2024. Students will research and create lanterns, dragons, and other symbols that represent the Chinese New Year. National Geographic Kids informative and comprehensive articles on the history of Valentine's Day which is well suited for elementary school children. Students can use their own cut out valentine hearts as math manipulatives in across-the-curriculum division and multiplication problems, the students can create their own Valentine cards and have a wonderful after school Valentine's party.

FEBRUARY — A 2024 CALENDAR

| SUNDAY | MONDAY | TUESDAY | WEDNESDAY | THURSDAY | FRIDAY | SATURDAY |
|--------|--------|---------|-----------|----------|--------|----------|
|  |  |  |  | 1 | 2 | 3 |
| 4 | 5 | 6 | 7 | 8 | 9 | 10 |
| 11 | 12 | 13 | 14 | 15 | 16 | 17 |
| 18 | 19 | 20 | 21 | 22 | 23 | 24 |
| 25 | 26 | 27 | 28 | 29 |  |  |

9

# MARCH

## LEPRECHAUNS & SHAMROCKS

Clutter-Free-Classroom is a great website that offers resources for teaching and celebrating holidays and events like Saint Patrick's Day, Women's History Month, Read Across America, and more for the elementary school level. Some art and reading activities that the students can choose include reading material about Ireland, leprechauns, and shamrocks.

After the teacher has taken the class for their library visit, the students can pick related books and write descriptive paragraphs about their favorite story. As an art activity which celebrates Saint Patrick's Day students can create their own designs by tracing and drawing shamrock patterns which can be cut out and pasted underneath their written paragraphs.

# MARCH

**A 2024 CALENDAR**

| SUNDAY | MONDAY | TUESDAY | WEDNESDAY | THURSDAY | FRIDAY | SATURDAY |
|--------|--------|---------|-----------|----------|--------|----------|
|        |        |         |           |          | 1      | 2        |
| 3      | 4      | 5       | 6         | 7        | 8      | 9        |
| 10     | 11     | 12      | 13        | 14       | 15     | 16       |
| 17     | 18     | 19      | 20        | 21       | 22     | 23       |
| 24     | 25     | 26      | 27        | 28       | 29     | 30       |
| 31     |        |         |           |          |        |          |

# APRIL

## FAVORITE CLOUD

Elementaryschools.science.com is a website which offers a lesson plan entitled Cloud 9. The Cloud 9 lesson plan teaches the students about the different types of clouds, how they are formed, and describes the characteristics of each type of cloud. After the class researches this material, students may choose their favorite cloud, write a short composition about why they chose their favorite cloud, and describe their cloud's characteristics. Following a class discussion, students can either draw, paint, or use cotton balls as an art activity to display their favorite cloud creations. This learning should conclude with the children attaching their creative cloud formations to be put beneath their short written compositions.

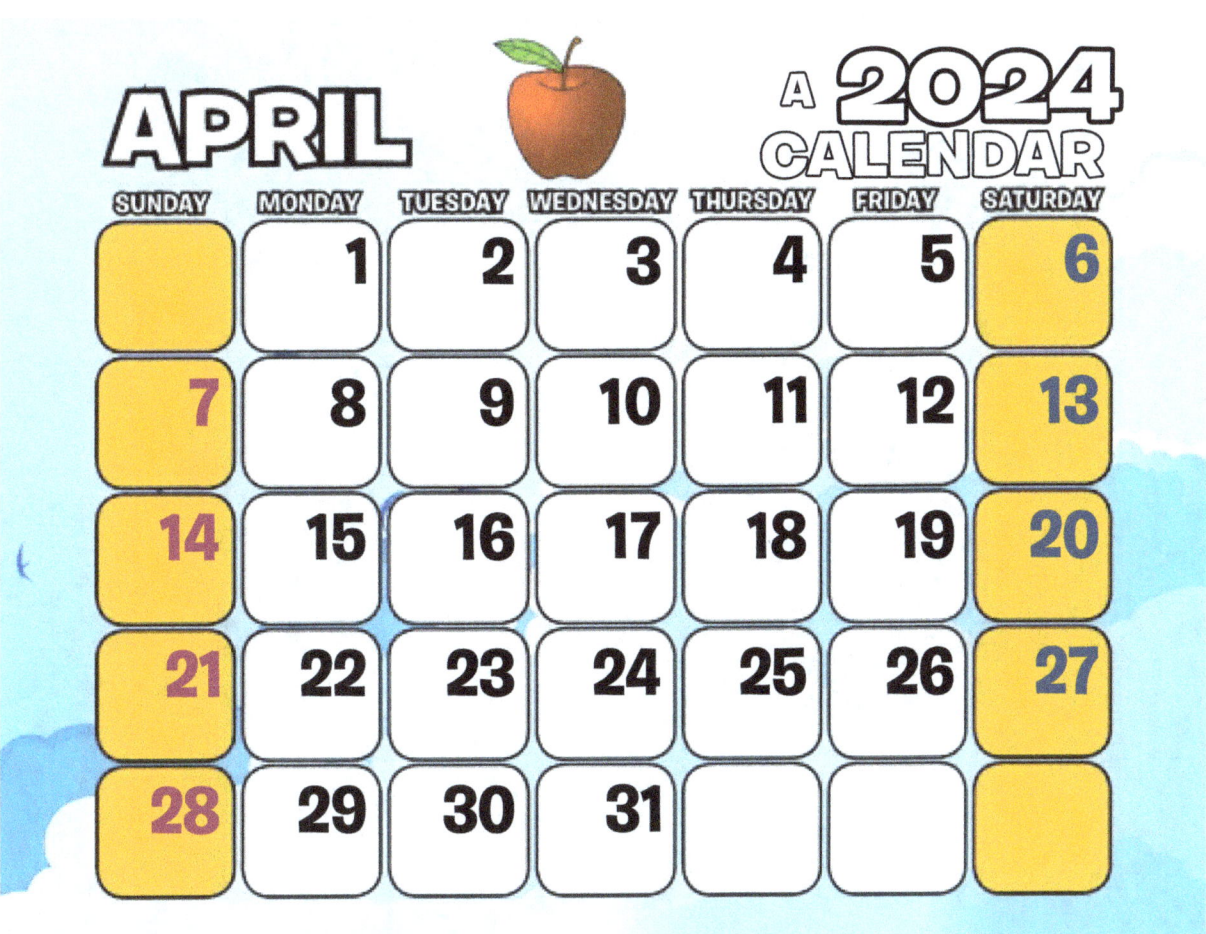

# APRIL

## A 2024 CALENDAR

| SUNDAY | MONDAY | TUESDAY | WEDNESDAY | THURSDAY | FRIDAY | SATURDAY |
|--------|--------|---------|-----------|----------|--------|----------|
|        | 1      | 2       | 3         | 4        | 5      | 6        |
| 7      | 8      | 9       | 10        | 11       | 12     | 13       |
| 14     | 15     | 16      | 17        | 18       | 19     | 20       |
| 21     | 22     | 23      | 24        | 25       | 26     | 27       |
| 28     | 29     | 30      | 31        |          |        |          |

# MAY

## MAY BRINGS FLOWERS

We Are Teachers is a website that has compiled a list of 18 classroom gardening ideas, lessons, tips and tricks that can help teachers help their students learn about plant life, plant cycles, botany, and ecosystems. They offer printables about the parts of a plant, anchor charts, and videos on plant life cycles. The teacher will give out handouts about this information on flowers and will encourage their students to draw the parts of a flower and label them. The teacher will engage the students in classroom discussions on the flowers and of each part of the flower. The teacher will model seed planting activities so that each student will know how to plant their flower seeds and they will be able to watch them grow, grow, and grow so that the children can take their plants home and put them in their own garden.

# MAY

## A 2024 CALENDAR

| SUNDAY | MONDAY | TUESDAY | WEDNESDAY | THURSDAY | FRIDAY | SATURDAY |
|---|---|---|---|---|---|---|
|  |  |  | 1 | 2 | 3 | 4 |
| 5 | 6 | 7 | 8 | 9 | 10 | 11 |
| 12 | 13 | 14 | 15 | 16 | 17 | 18 |
| 19 | 20 | 21 | 22 | 23 | 24 | 25 |
| 26 | 27 | 28 | 29 | 30 |  |  |

# JUNE

## MONARCH BUTTERFLY MIGRATION

KidWorldCitizen is a website which provides teachers and students a list of books, videos, and other resources that teachers can use to teach their students about the Monarch Butterfly migration. This website has valuable information on how to grow a school garden that will attract Monarch butterflies to promote continual learning during the summer break, teachers can encourage their students to visit their public library in order to engage in summer reading programs. As an inspirational topic students can access this other useful website to enhance their learning. http://www. monarch-butterfly.com is a wonderful website which could help inspire learners to gain more information about monarch butterfly migration and inspire the students to create the most beautiful butterfly drawings and paintings. Teachers can help students by working on having a public display of their art work in honor and display the students work.

# JUNE  A 2024 CALENDAR

| SUNDAY | MONDAY | TUESDAY | WEDNESDAY | THURSDAY | FRIDAY | SATURDAY |
|--------|--------|---------|-----------|----------|--------|----------|
|        |        |         |           |          |        | 1        |
| 2      | 3      | 4       | 5         | 6        | 7      | 8        |
| 9      | 10     | 11      | 12        | 13       | 14     | 15       |
| 16     | 17     | 18      | 19        | 20       | 21     | 22       |
| 23     | 24     | 25      | 26        | 27       | 28     | 29       |
| 30     |        |         |           |          |        |          |

# JULY

## THE RED, WHITE, AND BLUE AMERICAN FLAG

Larry Ferlazzo's website is a fantastic website that provides teachers with resources that can help students learn about the fourth of July. This website includes a special ESL Fourth of July lesson, a Fourth of July site from the History channel, and two resources from How Stuff Works that could be modified by teachers to make them more accessible to English Language Learners. The teacher will access the AmericanFlag.com website for students to explore colors, concepts of freedom, and symbols that represent the meaning of freedom. After the students learn about the concept of freedom and what each color represents, they may write a descriptive sentences about what freedom means to them. Students are challenged to create their own Fourth of July flag or Fourth of July Angel flag and employ the colors of red, white, and blue in the creations of their own designs.

| SUNDAY | MONDAY | TUESDAY | WEDNESDAY | THURSDAY | FRIDAY | SATURDAY |
|--------|--------|---------|-----------|----------|--------|----------|
|        | 1      | 2       | 3         | 4        | 5      | 6        |
| 7      | 8      | 9       | 10        | 11       | 12     | 13       |
| 14     | 15     | 16      | 17        | 18       | 19     | 20       |
| 21     | 22     | 23      | 24        | 25       | 26     | 27       |
| 28     | 29     | 30      | 31        |          |        |          |

# AUGUST

## BACK TO SCHOOL MAGIC BUS WORKSHEET

Teachers Pay Teachers is a website that offers a pack of Magic School Bus video Worksheets for every episode of the show. Each worksheet contains a single page guide that will keep the students engaged while learning and watching Mrs. Frizzle and her class head out on every exciting field trip.

On the first day of school students will get to design their own "Back To School Magic Bus" worksheet. Pictures of school buses will be handed out so that the students can design and create their own Back To School Magic Bus Worksheets. Now the students could record each students' name, address, name of their school, the principal, new teachers, and homerooms, etc. Each student could now record the date that they started back to school and make a list of new friends and old friends that they were glad to see on that day.

AUGUST

Back To School

A 2024 CALENDAR

| SUNDAY | MONDAY | TUESDAY | WEDNESDAY | THURSDAY | FRIDAY | SATURDAY |
|---|---|---|---|---|---|---|
|  |  |  |  | 1 | 2 | 3 |
| 4 | 5 | 6 | 7 | 8 | 9 | 10 |
| 11 | 12 | 13 | 14 | 15 | 16 | 17 |
| 18 | 19 | 20 | 21 | 22 | 23 | 24 |
| 25 | 26 | 27 | 28 | 29 | 30 | 31 |

# SEPTEMBER

## EXPLORING COLONIAL AMERICA

PBS-Thirteen is a website that provides a variety of resources for bringing Colonial America to life in the classroom. The lesson plans in this website provide a series of media rich lessons designed for immediate use in the classroom. Students will be encouraged to explore what life was like in Colonial America. They can engage themselves in learning through popcorn readings and choral readings in books about colonial life and break up into discussion groups of four. Each group will do both oral and written presentations Their presentations will highlight what interested them the most about colonial life. Underneath students' written work will be some of their artwork which might include depictions of their family members being transported in time to Colonial settings. The artwork that will be displayed under the students' written work will reflect a colorful, creative, rich, assortment of students' pictures and paintings.

# OCTOBER

## PUMPKINS, INDIANS, AND CORN HUSK DOLLS

Students will work together in groups of four by concentrating on solving addition and subtraction problems through the use of employing plastic pumpkin counters or candy corn counters as math manipulative learning tools. Student groups can conduct research and engage in pair-share reading by reading and sharing stories about pumpkins, indians, and corn.

Http://www.teachersfirst.com is a website that teachers can use to share with their students on how to make Native American Indian corn husk dolls step by step.

OCTOBER A 2024 CALENDAR

| SUNDAY | MONDAY | TUESDAY | WEDNESDAY | THURSDAY | FRIDAY | SATURDAY |
|--------|--------|---------|-----------|----------|--------|----------|
|        |        | 1       | 2         | 3        | 4      | 5        |
| 6      | 7      | 8       | 9         | 10       | 11     | 12       |
| 13     | 14     | 15      | 16        | 17       | 18     | 19       |
| 20     | 21     | 22      | 23        | 24       | 25     | 26       |
| 27     | 28     | 29      | 30        | 31       |        |          |

# NOVEMBER

## THE FIRST THANKSGIVING

Education World is a website project entitled "Teach The Real Story Of The First Thanksgiving" which includes an accurate telling of the first Thanksgiving starting with an accurate telling of the Plymouth Thanksgiving story. Education World includes study and discussion questions with ideas for enrichment, art projects, and authentic recipes. Students will read stories about the first Thanksgiving. They can discover and explore how Squanto and other Native American Indian tribes helped show the Pilgrims how to plant corn. Squanto showed the Pilgrims how to survive in their newly discovered land. Students can engage in TPR activities (Total Physical Responses) by putting on their own versions in a re-enactment of the first Thanksgiving. Students need to explore the different points of views that should come out in these discussions. Students could have a roundtable discussion as they need to consider and write about the different viewpoints among the Pilgrims and the Indians.

# NOVEMBER A 2024 CALENDAR

| SUNDAY | MONDAY | TUESDAY | WEDNESDAY | THURSDAY | FRIDAY | SATURDAY |
|--------|--------|---------|-----------|----------|--------|----------|
|  |  |  |  |  | 1 | 2 |
| 3 | 4 | 5 | 6 | 7 | 8 | 9 |
| 10 | 11 | 12 | 13 | 14 | 15 | 16 |
| 17 | 18 | 19 | 20 | 21 | 22 | 23 |
| 24 | 25 | 26 | 27 | 28 | 29 | 30 |

# DECEMBER

## PAPER SNOWFLAKES AND Q-TIP DESIGNS

The blog post titled "39 Fun ESL Games and Activities For An Exciting English Classroom" lists a variety of group activities that can be used to teach English in a fun and engaging way. The teacher will give out handouts on the winter season and snowflake formations. Students can engage in research about how snowflakes are formed and will choose the snowflake formation they would like to design. After engaging in class discussions students will work with their teacher as the teacher passes out papers on how students can fold their snowflake design papers into various symmetrical and asymmetrical patterns and be able to cut out their designs. The students can paste them on to various shades of blue construction paper to display in the classroom as a small winter art display to celebrate the winter season.